Haunted by Neil Armstrong

by
Neil Burns 2014

The author has published two books about his meetings with ghosts.

He has happy memories of winning a golf competition in 1969 with three strangers he met on a plane from Fiji to Honolulu. Other than one of them shared the name Neil, he could recall nothing about them.

However when Neil Armstrong died in 2012, an embargo put on them all at the Naval Base was lifted, and lots of memories started flooding back. The author began to wonder whether the other Neil might possibly be Neil Armstrong, the astronaut.

When he then realised that the date of the game had to be July 1969 and might be close to the date of the Moon landings, he began to get excited. He decided to return to Honolulu to retrace his steps and prove once and for all what happened.

Read how the author met Neil Armstrong's ghost several times and how he recalled with complete freedom what appears to the author to be the greatest military hoax of all time. Make up your own mind as to what actually happened.

Published by JocknDoris Publishers
ProseText@NeilBurns2014

ISBN No 978 0 9535748 3 4

Printed in England by
The Amadeus Press, Cleckheaton

Editing by
Alison Jane Norris

Photographs by
Neil Burns

For
JocknDoris Publishers
P O Box 112, Kidderminster
Worcs DY11 7SS

www.jockndoris.co.uk

*Dedicated to my four kittens who have been friends of mine all along
- Pretty, Biscuit, Houdini and Panic - all characters in their own
right. Only Biscuit and Panic are still with us after 14 years.*

Contents

Introduction
A Clean Sheet Of Paper

A clean sheet of paper - a fresh start.

Who could ask for more if they are planning to write a book?

Having just got the sad news from my friend Bernard from France, that he will not be joining me in the Calcutta Cup in September at St Andrews, I could be forgiven for being a bit depressed.

My only absolute and provable call to fame is winning the Calcutta Cup with my brother Robert in 1975 and that, after a dreadful struggle, not only against every other golfer we played against, but also against my delightful brother who was very stressful to play with, because he never ever said "Well played, Neil!" resulting in my standard family joke. Having put a very difficult 2 wood on the green, only 18 inches from the pin at the 17th on the New course, I rather hoped Robert would acknowledge that it might have helped us win the match, but all I heard was a grumble that I had left him a down hill putt!

I used to play really good golf in my younger days, particularly at University because I was fortunate enough to go to St Andrews - the "Home of Golf", because golf started there in the 1500's and has continued ever since. I was fortunate enough to be invited to join the Royal & Ancient Golf Club of St Andrews who administer the game worldwide and set the Rules of Golf. Many of the members are like myself now, in their later years and, as my wife rather cruelly pointed out, they are the reason for the term "Ancient" in the title. It is an honour to be a member and I have returned to play in their Autumn Meeting every year since 1969, when I became a member.

I had to fly from Cape Town where I lived in the seventies and take my two young sons, Andrew and Alastair, on the jumbo jet with me. I played in the knock out competitions and when my sons asked me each evening "Did you win today, Daddy?" I said with all modesty "Of course, yes indeed I did." They would then ask, "Where is the prize?" and I would reply that "The prize is playing again tomorrow on the greatest golf course in the world!"

I am only telling you this because the fact that I was a relatively good golfer is most relevant to later parts of this story. I played to a handicap of 2 for several years, in particular when I was at Royal Cape Golf Club where I was welcomed with open arms as they were struggling to put together a team for the inter club competition called the Stephan Trophy. I was delighted to play for the team and together with the Assistant Professional, David Wren, we managed to go from last in the league table, losing all our matches, to slowly climb up the table before winning it just before I moved on from the club. It was a lovely competition played on consecutive Sundays where the eight away teams met and played at the course of the ninth member. This had the very important effect of giving no-one the home advantage and all played on merit. There were no handicaps either, so you just had to beat the other chap all by yourself.

Chapter 1
First Ghost At Seventeen

I was born in Edinburgh in 1942, which now seems a long time ago.

My father was a farmer and spent a lot of his hard earned cash giving all of his four children a good education. I went to Loretto School in Musselburgh, arguably one of the finest public schools at that time. I enjoyed the learning process and finished with four A levels and 9 O levels but, because Modesty is my middle name, I am not going to tell you how good that is or was.

During that time I came across my first real ghost: the Lady in Grey at Pinkie Castle, and the story is told in Chapter 7 of my first book "A Few Special Ghosts I Have Met".

I was a boarder at the famous Loretto School in Musselburgh, just outside Edinburgh, and one term I was a Prefect in the House that was situated in Pinkie Castle. This contains the famous Painted Gallery - a room big enough to sleep 16 boys. It had a ceiling beautifully painted by some unknown artist, which captured the imagination as one lay in bed looking up at it.

I was lucky enough, however, to have my bed in Rest and Be Thankful, an amazing turret room only big enough for two, which I shared with a tough 17 year old called Beamy Smith - so called because he was a big lad and played front row in the rugby team.

This was a boys' public school. There were no girls at all. So it was a great surprise to me when, after lights out one evening early in the term, we saw the door to Rest and Be Thankful open and a tall, very feminine, slender figure in a long dress glide across to the window.

We were on the third floor and to get there you had to negotiate at least two rather tricky spiral staircases and it was right at the top corner of the Castle. The window itself was very small and, as I remember it, the wall of the turret was round so at best you would struggle to see very much out of the window.

But our guest was quite sure what she wanted to do and she moved about, constantly trying to get the best position to see out of the window.

She was clearly frustrated as she could make no progress and seemed in distress because her face showed a frown, not of hostility but of grief.

Who was this wonderful person? She was not a member of our school…

I lay in awe and considerable fear because this had to be a ghost I would have said, but - then again maybe not - so I decided to say nothing and wait a while.

Two or three days passed and again it happened. This time she arrived silently at the door and went across to the window to peer out into the dark, and then after ten minutes or so she would shrug her shoulders and return to the door with a look back as if to say, "I'll try again another time".

This time I noticed that it was not only a clear night but there was a strong moon. I couldn't remember if the conditions were the same the last time we saw her.

Then I wondered if Beamy had seen her too or maybe he was fast asleep?

"Are you awake?" I whispered.

"Yes", was the courageous reply. "I couldn't possibly sleep if the Lady of the Tower was here".

"Did you see her?" I asked.

"Of course I did – I was frightened that maybe you hadn't!"

"Whatever does she want and how can we help her?"

We decided, Beamy and I, that if we opened the window we might allow her to see more. But we were worried that she might jump out of the window, until we realised that the window was so small that she couldn't possibly get through.

We waited for nearly two weeks before we saw her again, but we had the window open every night - nearly freezing to death in the process. She did come back, and this time she looked right out the window and took off a headscarf, which was around her hair. She then cast it out of the window as if in the hope of catching something.

This was repeated time and again over the next few weeks, until we realised that the school term was nearly over. Our friend was less frustrated, but clearly still very unhappy.

One night right at the end of term, she threw her scarf so vigorously out of the window that she lost it. Both of us noticed that she had left without it about her head.

This made Beamy and I very excited because maybe we could find her scarf and return it to her.

The following morning we were both up with the larks and decided that an early morning run was called for. We set off round the castle but it wasn't as straightforward as you might imagine because there was a very high wall running one side which effectively split the castle surrounds in two.

One side was open to the windows of the Painted Gallery and the other to the windows of the Headmaster and his rooms…

Beamy and I, however, were determined and we sneaked round to the wall right under our turret window. We could not believe what we saw: there was the very same scarf! It had got caught in the old ivy which climbed up the wall. I retrieved it as fast as I could.

We only had that mystical scarf for one day because, that same night our Lady returned and found it where we had left it for her at the window.

She put it on and instead of walking straight to the door, she went to Beamy's bed and then mine to give us both a kiss on the forehead to say "thank you". I can still feel the warmth of those lips and the texture of the scarf to this day.

The reader may care to take note that the ghost of Pinkie is well documented. Apparently in 1760, Lady Elizabeth Seton of the house had a baby out of wedlock and in distress and confusion went to the turret and threw the little baby out of the tiny window to an accomplice outside.

She couldn't see properly and must have had the agony of not knowing whether her baby had been caught safely.

Had she thrown her scarf for us to find and demonstrate that there was a baby there?

We saw her a few more times later that term but on these occasions she was smiling: a little knowing smile, suggesting to us that she knew at last that her baby was fit and well and that at least was something.

Those of you who do not believe in ghosts should stop reading now because you will only become cross and frustrated. Please hand the book to a friend or neighbour, or do what one of the author's friends did with his first book, and put it in their downstairs loo for everyone else to read at their leisure.

Others will note that, as in every occurrence, the ghost appeared to the author at a place that she was known to have been and asked for his help either directly or in an obvious way.

Chapter 2
St Andrews University

I was delighted to get entrance to the University of my choice: St Andrews.

I went there in 1960 and spent the happiest years of my life attending lectures during the day and playing golf on the finest golf courses in the world.

In my final year of my BSc degree we heard that President Kennedy of America had challenged his fellow countrymen to send a man to the Moon and return him safely to Earth by the end of the decade. He also challenged all University students to carry out a 50-mile walk for charity. I took this up personally in that I joined the committee that organised a 55-mile walk from Stirling to St Andrews in 1963.

We challenged one of the American universities, called Union, to a contest over the walk. We organised 300 students with no specific training and on the day over a 100 of those finished the course in less than 24 hours. The boys from Union university put 60 trained athletes forward and they only achieved 15 of those finished! Their success rate was much lower than ours as a percentage.

As a final thesis for my Physics degree we were challenged by the legendary Professor Allen to write a paper entitled: Most difficult problems the Americans have to solve if they are to put a man on the Moon as challenged by their President.

I threw myself into this and wrote a good paper, which got me a good degree, and, again only because Modesty is my middle name, I will not tell you how good it was.

You are free to read it now, or go to the next chapter if you wish.

Suffice it to say the Professor gave me 17 ticks out of 20. He had a reputation for never giving full marks so I was kind of pleased with my 17.

You have two hours to state the twenty most difficult problems the Americans face if they are to put a man on the Moon by the end of the decade.

The Americans, known as the National Aeronautical and Space Agency (NASA), have successfully put several of their astronauts into orbit round the earth. No one as far as is known have ventured any further.

Therefore the challenge posed by their President is a monumental one and whilst we wish them every success it seems daunting at the outset.

The task of galvanising all the brains in the country to work on the task is in itself a hugely difficult thing to do and to come up with a plan that everybody can get behind is very difficult. The fact that there is a time limit on it only adds to the pressure.

They will already have data relating to the speed and direction of the craft they have used so far to get into orbit and those calculations are highly complex. The formulas and equations were first announced by Arthur C Clarke who is credited with working out the theory relating to orbiting craft. In essence there are conflicting forces at work on any craft from the bodies closest to them by way of gravity. Their craft will experience a significant gravitational pull towards the earth and unless some other force counters that, it will crash to the ground.

Depending on its speed, there will be a centrifugal force which will drive it outwards away from the earth and this is directly proportional to the speed of the craft.

Clarke worked out that, at a speed of around 15,000 mph that force would be equal to the gravitational force if the craft was around 150 miles from the earth.

Unless and until these forces balance the craft will carry on towards outer space but when they do balance the craft will go into a near circular orbit round the earth.

The difficulty of calculating would require computing power and is only possible if all the basic information is available. It would seem that any craft would therefore require a computer on board to allow the crew to perform their next calculation.

Whilst this is theoretically possible the current size and weight of computers is very heavy and could not be carried unless the craft is very big.

The second difficulty is that the speed at which the craft must travel must be precisely accurate otherwise it will miss its orbit or crash to the ground unless some in flight adjustment is made and NASA have no experience of this as far is known.

The assumption is that once the craft is in orbit it will be given a boost by an on board motor at precisely the right amount and direction so that it heads precisely towards the Moon. Bearing in mind the complexity of the calculations required it would appear that the chances of doing that are extremely low.

Currently NASA have a huge rocket called a Saturn which stands at its launch pad 13 stories high and is almost entirely full of fuel. The problems they have experienced to date relate to the force that they know they have to exert to absorb the massive weight of the fuel so that the whole craft can rise from the launch pad.

Unless some new way can be found to propel the initial boost it seems logical that the problem will be exacerbated rather than eased by the necessity to take a much bigger craft to the moon. One astronaut has been flown but now we must assume that they are going to provide for a multi-crew which require to carry with them some craft ready to return them to earth which of course was one of the criteria laid down by President Kennedy. It seems most unlikely that they will solve this problem.

Although little is known of the environment they will find in transit to the moon there is likely to be radiation from space which is hostile in the extreme and they will also be subject to that when they step on to the moon so they will require very heavy protective clothing in their suits to protect them from these dangers which they can't specify at this stage.

If they were to get to the moon they will require to get back again into orbit and as the speed required to obtain orbit round the moon is 15,000mph it will require a massive force to propel the mooncraft back into orbit. The force required is beyond comprehension and the G forces experienced would be massive and probably fatal to the astronauts on board.

They then have to join up with the mothercraft which is itself travelling at a huge speed and the chances of them achieving a link up are minimal. Trials have been carried out on earth between two vehicles on a flat road with no other complications and it is nearly impossible to pass an object from one vehicle to another even in the simplest circumstances.

Disorientation would be something the astronauts would have to suffer - like the giddiness suffered after being spun on a fairground wheel. The astronauts would require a major amount of training to become adept at this and of course it is not possible to recreate those circumstances on earth.

One assumes that the craft will be in constant communication with the base. It will take a significant amount of time to radio or equivalent signal to be sent and returned. The time taken will be a major disadvantage in trying to control the craft or give assistance to the crew. It is noted that for certain periods the craft will be on the far side of the moon and totally out of contact with its base, so will have to fend for itself.

Unless all the calculations are performed in advance and go according to plan then there are bound to be some calculations that cannot be performed with disastrous consequences.

The last problem to highlight is almost certainly the biggest.

It is possible to calculate the percentage chance of any event happening and in Statistics there are formulas for working out the overall chances for success in a mission. It is most unlikely that the percentage chance is 100% on any one occurrence and a more realistic assessment would be 90%. If there are more than a few critical points in the mission and they are all at 90% then the percentage chance drops by 90% each time to 81% 73% 64% and so on.

In the complex mission which the astronauts will have to undertake there must be dozens of critical points and not all of those have a high chance of success.

Regrettably therefore the chances become lower and lower the more complex the venture and chances become almost negligible. It seems that they would be so slim that it might be impossible to persuade any astronaut to take them on, because disaster is almost inevitable.

All of the above is from memory straight down on to paper.

Chapter 3
Edinburgh To Cape Town

I next headed for Edinburgh because, unknown to me, my father had arranged an apprenticeship with a firm of Chartered Accountants in Melville Crescent and I was indentured for the princely sum of £1,400 over a period of five years, reduced to three and a half years because I had a BSc degree.

I thoroughly enjoyed some more learning. I lived in Bruntsfield in a flat with my sister Frances and settled into the Edinburgh way of life quite well, taking a number 16 bus down Lothian Road every morning hoping it would be there to take me back that night.

During that time I quite literally bumped in to a lovely girl called Lesley and knocked her over to the ground on a zebra crossing at the bottom of Lothian Road.

Of course I was distraught and had to help pick her up and offer to escort her back to her flat, which was in Athol Crescent. One thing led to another and then she told me six months later that she was finishing her physiotherapy course and heading back to Cape Town where she lived. I found out that there was a special rule for Chartered Accountants that in exceptional circumstances they could have their indentures transferred to another Scots CA in practice overseas for a maximum of 6 months.

So, full of confidence, I told Lesley that I was planning to come across to Cape Town and she wasn't going to escape me so easily!

The year was 1965 and commercial aeroplanes were in their infancy. The leaders in the field were the VC10 and the Comet. I booked a flight to Cape Town but it straddled three days. We flew only to Tenerife on the first flight and stayed in a hotel there overnight.

After a leisurely breakfast, we returned to the airport to take off for a further two flights to Cape Town. Whether we went first to Johannesburg or direct to Cape Town it doesn't really matter because I arrived wearing my kilt to lay down my credentials. I also brought my putter with me because I didn't trust the airport handlers with such a valuable and breakable item. My prospective father in law was a Scot through and through, so the kilt went down well and later when we got married in 1966 I was wearing my kilt of course. During my speech I admonished my new bride Lesley of tugging at my kilt and I wondered what she was indicating and, as I remember it, that brought the house down.

We had a lovely honeymoon going up the Garden Route recommended to anybody even if they aren't on honeymoon! We returned to Cape Town to fly back to Edinburgh because I had some exams to sit. Rather fortunately the Taxation exams were on Corporation Tax and Capital Gains Tax, both of which were new to everybody including, I am told, our lecturer at the Institute.

Rather surprisingly I passed the exam and was very glad of that. Lesley and I then moved into the flat in Bruntsfield Avenue which was very obligingly vacated by my sister and we had a happy 18 months or so until I qualified in 1967.

I had promised my accounting boss that if I decided to return to Cape Town I would be very happy to come and work for him for the first year. This suited us both admirably as I had a good job to go to and he had a fully qualified CA to do his auditing work for him. Some people would find the auditing a bit dull and so I only stayed the mandatory year with Syfrets.

I played a lot of golf in those days and got my handicap down to 2, which required a lot of effort to maintain. I joined Royal Cape Golf Club where my father-in-law was a member and enjoyed the golf immensely.

The first job that I found was with Mercantile Holdings Ltd in Buitenkant Street and that was also where I saw my next ghosts, as told in the next story originally published in my first book: "A Few Special Ghosts I Have Met".

Buitenkant Street, Cape Town was where the warehouse was.

I enjoyed my spell as an Accountant at Mercantile Holdings but soon it was time to move on and I found a super job at Coates Brothers a subsidiary of a company based in London who had their offices in Maitland a suburb of Cape Town.

Chapter 4
Out To Auckland

I had been headhunted by their Cape Town office because I was a Chartered Accountant who had flair for the early computer programmes. Being interested enough to write my own programmes in Quick Basic, I became Chief Accountant and Company Secretary and had a fine office in Maitland and an even finer car. Cars in those days were a status symbol, and as I was supposed to be a quite important person, I was given a Chevrolet Constantia to drive. It was American and enormously wide, so much so that there seemed to be enough room for 3 people across the continuous front seat.

It had to be bigger than the car driven by any of the Salesmen but not of course as grand as that driven by the Managing Director or Chairman.

I studied the accounting systems currently used by the company and found them to be just about adequate. Almost all had hand written ledgers and invoicing and were very staff labour intensive and gave really no useful information to management. There was even a Private Ledger, which contained we know not what! They were crying out for a mechanised accounting system for invoicing and producing the statistics required to assist the various buying and production departments.

When I suggested this should be done I was told that they already had a good system in Auckland and so by far the best thing to do was for me to go there and study their methods and bring back the best bits to install in Cape Town.

It was during this time early in 1969 that I was sent by my company Coates Brothers (South Africa) Ltd to Auckland in New Zealand to study their computer and accounting systems. They were the leading company in the world making inks of all kinds ranging from rotary black for newspaper printing to thick white paint for the lines marking the centre of the road.

So I was supplied by London Head Office with an around-the-world Air Ticket which was the most economical way of travelling long distances in those days. It was much cheaper than buying several tickets between the various airports and provided you carried on round the world in the same direction the ticket was valid. I was instructed by our Managing Director to go to Auckland, stay as long as I needed to gather the information, and return with it in due course.

I went east to Johannesburg, then Bombay, then Singapore, and on to Perth and then Sydney and eventually to Auckland. When I arrived, exhausted, I was welcomed in a very friendly way by Roger Manuel, their Managing Director. As a welcome to Auckland he had a lovely surprise - tickets for an orchestral concert in the Town Hall that night. I had just time to change before they took me to the concert where I had to prop my eyes open I was so desperate for sleep. I remember counting the number of violinists, and the number of trumpeters, and then counting the choir at the back, and am almost certain I caught the eye of one of the tall and rather attractive sopranos - suffice it to say they delivered me back to my hotel on Mount Eden, and I collapsed into sleep without unpacking my suitcase.

The Hotel was a sort of boarding house on the upper slopes of Mount Eden which is near the centre of Auckland, and you can look over the whole city from there. I enjoyed my stay there and got to know the staff quite well. It was only a short drive to the Coates Brothers Factory and Office, and they gave me one of the salesman's cars.

On the first day I was grateful to follow Roger's grand car to the Office.

I had rather assumed that they would give me large office and at least one secretary, but Roger said that before you do anything you must learn to make ink. So he gave me a sort of boiler suit which zipped up the middle to the chin, and I was sent to the production department to decant concentrated dyes, resins and chemicals from the drums in which they had just arrived by sea from London. The method adopted by the company was to make all the formulations in London, and then send the concentrate which matched exactly the right colour and texture, out to the distant outposts.

There was therefore complete consistency for, let's say, Dunhill, so their unique light purple ink used on all their packs of cigarettes, would be the same on all other products famous throughout the world. Absolutely critical that it was, day in day out, year in year out, exactly the same colour and of course, that it could not fade in the sun, or change in any way because then all the cigarettes would have be destroyed.

I had to open up one of the bigger drums sent from London and decant it into much smaller tins and that had to be precisely weighed so that there was no overage or under and by far the most important, no wastage. I vividly remember my arm aching vigorously as I tried to get out the last tiny bit of concentrate in the crack at the bottom of the drum. Whatever you do there is always some left. Now waste in ink making has be controlled absolutely and has a huge effect on the costs. If wastage is too high and part of the reason why Roger Manuel insisted I did the decanting was to stress how difficult it was, and still is, to get the last bit out of any barrel, be it ink or something nice like syrup where the last bit to get out is sometimes worth getting. Eventually I got the last bit out and the production boys escorted me to Roger Manuel's office, still of course in my boiler-suit, which was by this time covered in every colour imaginable, and my boots were caked with all manner of things from the production floor. "I can't go into the Managing Director's office like this" I said, and they all cried that was what he insisted you do. I went into Roger's office and he burst into laughter because he knew that his plan had worked.

To this day I know that wastage is a most important part of the cost of making anything, and in ink particularly so. In every retail shop there is wastage, and very often pilferage, which has to be added in to the final cost of sales, and if it is allowed to get out of hand then not only do you lose control, but you lose profit as well.

I was sent to the showers and eventually emerged in the office suit I had so carefully packed to bring with me. I was shown how the accounting systems worked, and how the cost of every ink made, was built up from a formula of the recipe of each ink formulated to one hundredth of a percent, but added to that was a precise figure for wastage, and I nodded very wisely when that was explained to me.

The systems were excellent and interlinked, so that whenever an order was received for pillar box red ink, a detailed analysis of the constituent parts was produced and sent to the stock room, to check that every part was available and of course if even one constituent part was out of stock, it was a disaster as it couldn't be produced.

The statistics that their system produced, gave a forecast of the usage of all inks and concentrates, and of course this not only allowed the buying department to order ahead, and make sure that we had enough stock, but gave them buying power knowing precisely the volume required.

These statistics also gave an accurate cost of each order, to see what profit this made, allowing of course for an appropriate amount for wastage. When eventually I left I was treated to a wonderful dinner paid for from a secret fund or kitty, which turned out to be concentrates recovered from the bottom of drums by people like Neil Burns, and I found out that we had overages from several of the drums I had emptied but, of course, they were not going to tell me at the time!

Chapter 5
Fly To Fiji And Then Honolulu

Roger Manuel ran me to the Airport at Auckland and I was rather touched to notice that, about six of the staff I had got to know during my short stay, also came along.

It had been a very happy period, probably because the job I came to do was easy in that all the hard work had already been done by some very nice people at Coates Brothers.

I had a briefcase bulging with papers and sample documents, ready to show my team in Cape Town when I got back, but I had to get there first. I had been given an around-the-world ticket, and the rules stated that provided I kept going round the world the same way I could carry on flying. I looked at the map and having come in to Auckland going east I had to keep going east.

I plotted a course, which took me firstly to Fiji then Honolulu and then across to Los Angeles and then New York, London and Cape Town. There weren't flights everyday so I had to resign myself to being forced to stop over in some if not all of these places at, I may say, the expense of whichever Airline was fortunate enough to be responsible for me on that part of the journey.

At the airport in Auckland I checked in at the Fiji Airways desk. The elegant airhostess confirmed that there was room for me on the flight going out at 10am local time. In maybe five or six hours I should be landing in Fiji, and there was another flight onward to Honolulu where a seat had been reserved for me. I would have to stop over for a minimum of two days, before the next flight with an American Airline which would take me on to Los Angeles, when I would then become their problem.

We had an early lunch on the flight to Fiji and some rather nice wine, which meant sleeping was not a problem in the afternoon. There were only a dozen people on the plane and most of them got off at Fiji. It was a pity I didn't have time to explore Fiji as we only stopped for two hours, and so I carried on straight to the check-in counter from the baggage collection area.

Someone told me in a loud voice that my clubs were being taken separately and this was reassuring because I would be lost without my favourite golf clubs. There is always an anxious wait on the plane before you take off but we had clearly waited longer than normal when the Captain announced that we are going to wait a few minutes longer because we are giving a lift to three passengers who have just arrived unexpectedly by boat. He couldn't give any more information and whilst this rather annoyed us, it sparked our curiosity.

Eventually, three men in their early thirties came aboard, obviously part of a team as they clearly knew each other, and whilst one of them kind of apologised to us as they went up to the front section of the plane, the other one was muttering about "a dreadful way to treat anyone" and he was clearly unhappy.

When we eventually took off the airhostess could throw no further light on it but reassured me in a loud voice that my golf clubs were most definitely aboard.

The three men went right up the front on the plane with the air hostess telling them that they would be comfortable up there.

Because we were travelling east catching up with the clock, we then proceeded to have another lunch and I am not ashamed to tell you that I enjoyed a very similar lunch to the earlier one and had some more of that very fine wine. After the mandatory after lunch snooze I went for a walk as I always do round the plane. I am usually able to find the little nook the staff use for preparing the meals and very often they have a stash of soft drinks and chocolates and sure enough there was a tray already set out on the counter. "Help yourself," a notice said so I enjoyed a chocolate bar and some tropical fruit juice which I might otherwise not have been offered.

As I was standing there, one of the three newcomers came towards me saying that those looked good, and of course I offered him a choice from the tray. The juice we both thought was mango and particularly good, and we helped ourselves to some more which we found in the little fridge inset into the cupboard there. With a wave of his hand my new friend called across to his friends to come and see what we had found.

We stood like schoolboys who had found the secret tuck box and congratulated ourselves on our good luck. Eventually we got chatting and they asked me what I was doing and seemed quite interested in my story saying that I didn't look like a Chartered Accountant, which I took as a compliment. "You do play golf, however", and I had to agree. One of them claimed that I was off a low handicap and, I couldn't deny that to be the truth.

MAP OF WORLD - WEST

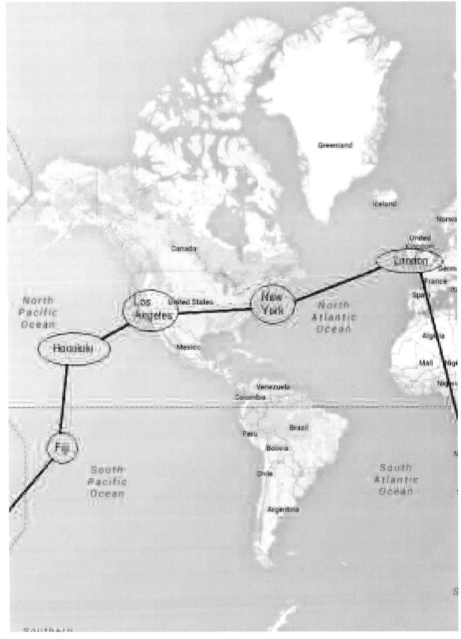

MAP OF WORLD - EAST

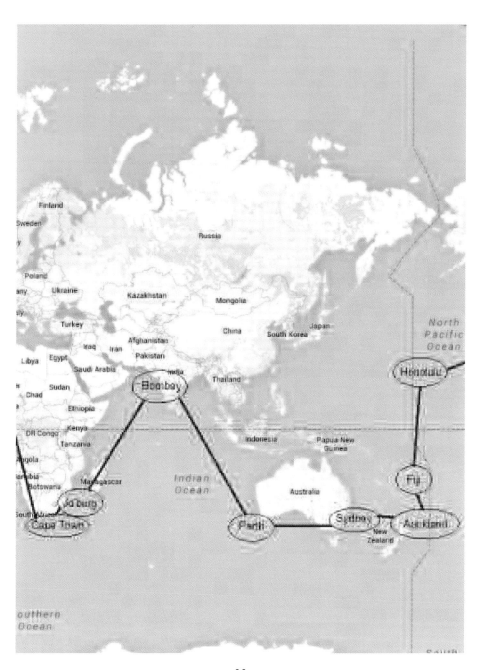

Naturally I asked them what they were doing and they said they were in the military but couldn't tell me what they did because it was a bit secret.

"All we are allowed to do is training and simulated exercises which we are fed up with and how we wish we could go and do the real thing. If we win the golf tomorrow we will show you round our training ground."

We must have been there chatting for half an hour when the air hostess eventually broke up the party scolding us for drinking all the Mango juice on the plane! The fact that we all said it was particularly good didn't seem to placate the lady at all.

It was a slightly longer flight this one but we still landed in the light and were told that we would be transferred to the Airport Hotel by a little shuttle bus sent for the purpose.

"That suits us all perfectly – you go and have a good nights sleep we want you on good form for tomorrow", said one of three, "We will arrange to pick you up to go to Navy Marine in the morning about 8 - will that do?"

"Have you got your gear with you?" they asked and I said, "Yes indeed I have the gear I wear in South Africa".

I used to wear long shorts in South Africa with, of course, long socks - very smart and polished as I was a member of Royal Cape Golf Club and dress was always smart. Caddies were on hand and your clubs would have been cleaned and shoes polished. As I looked down at my feet I noticed immediately how shiny my shoes were and the socks were to just below the knee. My shorts were long by today's standard but I recognised them and I was wearing my trademark waistcoat, which I always wore over my golf shirt. And of course as I was playing every week, the part just above and below the knee was heavily tanned which looked ridiculous when having a shower. Everyone was the same of course!!

When I joined them at the Navy Marine Club to play in the competition all of us were wearing shorts. The three others were all the same, noticeably so, and I commented:

"You fellows look very smart and part of a team" and one of them whisked me inside and said to the Club Pro "We want to look our best today so please give this chap a fine pair of shorts and charge to my account."

I thought that was a marvellous gesture and as he was helping me into them in a hidden corner of his shop he said "Don't worry sir I will parcel these up for you nicely and let you have them back at the end of the round". Whilst I was checking that I had tees and markers and pitch marker repairer, the Professional said "if the man is paying for these shorts you better have a few of his balls, where you will notice they are all marked with a big N for ease of identification". I put them straight into my bag and have put an N for Neil on my golf balls ever since!

I felt really good in the outfit because I felt part of a team and I think they did too and when we got going in the round and they realised how far I hit the ball, they tried to point this out to all the others. Sometimes I had to wait a little on the tee because it is rude to drive into the players in front which you can do sometimes but only if you hit a much better than expected drive.

Chapter 6
Competition Won!

I was picked up from the Ohana Hotel promptly at 8am and taken the very short distance to the Navy Marine course. Apparently the competition was like a Texas Scramble, which could be great fun particularly if you used your head as well as your clubs.

All four players drive and you must choose just one of those to continue. You put a tee down close to your ball and that person must play the next shot first followed by the other three from the same position. You then walk forward, and take the next crucial decision as to which ball to choose. Very often it is very obvious but sometimes a little thought should be taken. Each player must have at least four drives taken and it is best to take these early rather than late because it eases the pressure. If you have only had two of your drives taken by the 14th, let's say, then pressure comes on to hit a good drive and that pressure can play on the mind of any player.

Also it is not always right to play the ball nearest to the hole because that may have to go over something like a bunker, which again causes unnecessary stress.

The first hole was a relatively easy par four, where most golfers would get on in two shots. It was Michael's honour and he did us proud by hitting a good one down the middle. With that in the bank, I could try and hit a long drive to give us the advantage of length and the other three could then have the distance with the second shot to reach the green. This worked out well and we all played up and got a four.

I had to keep a record of which drives we had used and the other Neil had not had any drives up to the fourth so that when, at the fifth, he hit a reasonable one I judged it would be better to take his rather than mine just to get him on the scoreboard. I made up for that by hitting a wonderful second off the other Neil's ball to the heart of the green. The others were warming to this and we started planning some strategic putts. At this hole we were twelve yards away in two, and we agreed to have the first putt as a sighter. I played it and it finished two inches to the left of the hole. We marked that and encouraged the other three to go for the putt aiming exactly two inches right. The first one unfortunately was slightly too hard and slid past but the last one with no pressure went straight in the hole. We had our first birdie!

We carried on like that and got mostly pars with a couple of rescue shots needed from me but most of the good golf coming from the others because there was no pressure.

We finished the round in 68 having had four birdies, three of them at the short holes, which are by definition the easiest, and the other at a par five where I got two really long shots on the green having had to use my drive.

When we came off to report to the starter we could hear the pre-match favourites already having a celebratory beer in the clubhouse / changing room. When we had our card checked by the starter he was most impressed: "No disasters at all and three of you are off 28". He made the appropriate deductions for handicap and we were the best by three strokes. "You have won the free trip to Mauna Kea - you will enjoy that!" So it was time for us to have a celebratory beer and offer to buy one for the others who we had just pipped.

As we were getting ready to head off to Mauna Kea someone from the Military Base came across to us and said "I hope you fellows are not forgetting that you will need to get back to base very soon because you have to be ready to be collected. I know you would rather play golf than go to the Moon but you are expected !!!"

The other three looked at one another and shrugged their shoulders, " Yes, we would not have enough time to go across and back again, so we will have to take a rain check on Mauna Kea. Don't worry Neil", they said to me, "we will just put it on hold and the next time you come back to Honolulu we will go over to Kona and claim our prize."

I was extremely disappointed as I think we all were, but it seemed quite important and I said "As long as you promise to put it on hold for the next time I will be back !!!"

I didn't know then that I would have to wait over 40 years before claiming my prize, but it explains the reason that I have been apprehensive about playing golf ever since, never knowing quite why.

My three new friends set off for their own lodgings, which I think, were in the Navy Base Camp. I went back to the Hotel, where the receptionist asked where we had been. I was lost for words and couldn't think. She said "Don't worry many people have the same problem - I suggest a nice swim in the pool and you will be right as rain".

I went into the changing room there and was given a pair of hotel swimming trunks while they took my other clothes "We'll give these a bit of an iron", said the girl "ready for you after your dip." it seemed everybody was plotting my path ahead.

When I went back to reception to say how much I had enjoyed the dip and asked where the other three were she said, "I am not sure who you mean, but there is a message for you that your flight to Los Angeles has been booked for 6pm tonight and our buggy will take you there. You will have to hurry. One of our girls has packed your suitcase and it is all ready with your clubs."

"What about my bill?" I asked.

"Oh, that is paid for by the airline because you have an around-the-world ticket", and that was that. Before I could draw another breath I was on the buggy and scooting away to the airport.

As I was shouting a goodbye the girl shouted back "See you again" with a sort of knowing look, and I looked forward to that very much indeed.

History

History records that Neil Armstrong and his two colleagues took off in their Saturn V rocket from the Kennedy Space Centre on July 16 1969, with over a million people sitting on the ground watching. It must have been the most exciting event in most people's experience.

They splashed down in North Pacific Ocean on July 24 1969 with the whole world watching, and everyone was delighted they landed safely proving that achieved the goal set out by their President J F Kennedy.

However this also left them ample time to carry out their planned hoax by arranging an early splashdown a little further south, with absolutely nobody watching on 20 July 1969, when they accompanied the author back to Honolulu.

The easiest place to hide, if no one is looking for you, is out in the open and what better place than the 14th fairway at Navy Marine Golf Club!

Chapter 7
Back To Cape Town

Thank goodness I sleep well on planes. I had a very long flight across to New York where we rested up a little before crossing to London and later all the way down to Cape Town. I was booked all the way through and as they never leave a passenger behind I was confident we would make it.

As promised, I sent a cable from New York and hoped that my team would collect me from the airport. Sure enough, Lesley brought Andrew to meet his internationally travelling Dad. Of course, all I had was my suitcase packed by the girl in Mauna Kea and my golf clubs, and when I got those home and opened up the bag to make sure my shoes were clean enough for the next game, I found a scorecard from Mauna Kea signed by my three friends saying "Look forward to playing with you again".

Lesley said that I had been picked to play at Rondebosch against Mowbray in the Stephan Trophy. "But before that you had better come with me!" called out George Allardyce who was my boss, "We want to see those papers you have brought back from Auckland."

As soon as I had cleared my suitcase through customs they insisted I open it up. There was my briefcase inside the main suitcase with the file and the folder and all the memories of those systems that I had been studying flowed back.

In the meantime I had some systems to install at Coates Brothers and that was both a challenge and a pleasure. I got in touch with Peter at Burroughs and started the process of ordering the Burroughs accounting machines which had a rather complicated bar across the front and top which controlled the mechanism below so that we could have a separate bar to allow invoicing to be done on pre-printed invoices on a long continuous roll. The girls would type in a customer number and we were amazed to see the machine print out the address details. The girl then entered the code number of the ink ordered and the quantity and it rattled off the price and the total.

Another line and another ink and it rattled again and then she would press the total button and the invoice was totalled and printed much to the amazement and delight of our girl.

At the end of the day we had a routine that produced a punched paper tape which was a continuous roll with loads of holes at strategic points. This was put in an envelope ready for Peter to collect at 5pm and take away to his computer bureau. He would return at 9am the next morning with statistics showing how much we had sold, analysed between all the different inks, but far more importantly, it showed how much stock of concentrates and resins had been used, broken down and summarised ready to be sent to the buyers department to make sure the stock re-order was placed.

Previously, all the sales invoices were written out by the sales department and typed onto company letterheads with carbon paper for a permanent record. A girl would write the totals into the Sales Day Book which would have to be added up and then the totals written each day in the Nominal ledger. How much profit had been made we didn't know until at the end of the quarter, when a stock take would reveal the cost of materials, which again would be put into the nominal ledger. There was a purchase Day Book where all purchases were hand written and eventually analysed in the ledger. A Trial Balance would be drawn to check it was all correct, and of course self-balancing and then this trial balance would go to the Chief Accountant who would prepare the accounts and show the profit.

Of course, because there were invariably some distorting factors, the Chief Accountant would make his own secret adjustment to make sure the figures made the Chairman happy, London happy, and eventually the shareholders on the Johannesburg Stock Exchange happy - quite a balancing act and that was why he was paid a good salary and had very nice car.

This caused great excitement, but it took a little time and a great struggle to get to that stage. We had all the names and addresses to put in and the formulas which were of course on a punched paper tape which had flown with me from Auckland to Fiji to Honolulu and we of course learned how to re-input those figures with most accurate ones and create all our own statistics.

"What about the wastage?" I hear you cry. We were able to take regular stock takes and produce our own wastage tables which I would send to Roger Manuel to compare with his and challenge for the top spot in the keep-wastage-down table.

The whole trip was enormously beneficial to Coates Brothers as it brought the accounting procedures a giant leap forward and later people from our sister company in India were sent to learn from us how to produce their own paper tape.

My Chevrolet car had been looked after and I took the whole family to the next match at Rondebosch and when David Wren asked me where had I played recently I told him about Navy Marine and the three men from Honolulu.

We drove back to Constantia to our house called Cambusmuir and my wife told me that Maria, our maid, had helped her with watering the hedge at the top. "If we had known it was going to be so much work we would never have let you go away", she said.

It was only a few months later that we had the dreadful earthquake in Tulbagh which registered 6.5 on the Richter scale on 29 September 1969 and it was just as well I was there to get our son Andrew out into the car for safety. The quake was many miles away but still strong enough to have caused some damage to the structure of the building including a great crack through the steps outside the front door.

"Did you play any golf when you were away?" I hear someone ask!

Chapter 8
Stepping Stone In Time

This short middle section of the book is put here as a small stepping-stone for all my readers to pause for a few moments in time.

The chapters you have just read were all set in 1969 and can be looked at as a complete story. The following set of chapters are all set in 2013, which for sake of argument is the present day as this is written.There is a huge gap of 44 years between the two, and in order for you to appreciate how much that is, I am setting you down gently in 1990 first.

That was just twenty-one years onwards and a time I remember well as a very happy time. I practised as a Chartered Accountant in Coventry Street Kidderminster and my office was run by a splendid girl called Alison. We could always rely on Alison to have the done the job that I should have done - all the filing and the telephone calls and keeping us right. She was also a wizard on the new computers which were coming in. We were the Agents for Tandon Computers of Redditch who made theirs locally. They were new and state of the art.

My main task was submitting people's Tax Returns and I would have to send one in for every client I had. There were no computers for individuals so every one had to be hand written on the dreaded Tax Return that had to be in by the 31 January each year without fail.

I would sometimes have a queue of clients on the last three days with us scrambling to put together figures into their returns. Alison would very efficiently take a note of all the figures in the pre-laid out schedule we had. No photocopiers of course in those days and it was a total disaster if you didn't know what figures you had sent in if the Inland Revenue asked you for them.

The post we used to receive in February was always exciting, never dull. We had a mixture of the rude letters from the Revenue levying a fine of £100 for not sending a return in and they accepted no excuses - I know because I have tried them all (including "Alison forgot to post them!"). We did however receive some letters which were on a pale yellow paper, which you could see through the window envelope, and these were almost always a refund which was terribly good news.

I can throw myself back to that time easily and visualise my office and Alison looking as attractive as ever. We had just written a series of programs using QuickBasic, a very straight forward programing language and I was able to offer my clients "Custom Build Computer Programs our Speciality". They all went under the Jockndoris banner and one of those clients still runs the programs successfully today. I remember being helped at that time by Simon who worked for us and Martin Evans who wrote many programs from his faraway cottage in Wales.

I had a swish car and had one of the first car phones, where there was a quite sizeable box in the passenger department and a long aerial, and if you were lucky you could make a phone call locally to impress your fellow passengers.

This world was 20 years later than the world you have just left in 1969 but you would notice the dramatic moves forward in technological ability between the two. Things possible in this world had been quite unthinkable in 1969.

Soon I am going to throw you forward into the next chapters set in 2013, and you can now take with you your mobile phones and laptop computers. I took both of mine with me to Honolulu and connected with WiFi to check my emails when I got to the other side of the world. None of those were available in 1990 and had never been thought of way back in 1969.

Why bother with ghosts you may ask ?

Those of you who have reached this stage all profess to believe in ghosts as I do. That is because I see them fairly regularly although I am quite unable to explain why.

Clearly I have an affinity for them and they know that I will be able to see them. Whether that is because I go back in time to be with them I don't know.

Every ghost that I have ever seen has appeared at the appropriate age for the place visited. If I take the trouble to look and see, I too was at the age I would have been had I gone back in time to that place.

I have been back to Fontainebleau near Paris on many occasions, and I make life easy for them by wearing Tudor clothes. The sceptics among you will say that makes it too easy but I want to invite the young Mary Queen of Scots to appear and to ask for help if she chooses.

If young Mary shows me the secret garden then I am always dressed in rather scruffy gardeners clothes. If I look carefully enough my hands and nails show that what I do every day, work as a gardener called Jacques le jardinièr who was part of Mary Queen of Scots entourage in the 1570's.

I would like to make this book useful to those who read it. If I can explain to any one of you how I go back in time then that might help you to go back in time as well. Provided of course that you want to do so. Some of us are frightened to go back because we might get stuck there, and not able to return and that was the fear of my late wife Jennifer.

I was concerned when I went back to Hawaii that that would happen to me, so much so that I left instructions in the top drawer of my desk for my sons to deal with matters if I did not come back. The notes included all my passwords to the websites some of them critically important others not so much so but vital nevertheless.

In the event I did come back and my precautions were unfounded but the piece of paper is still there.

I constantly have a fear before I play golf about lots of things, my clothes, my clubs my shoes and most often that I will be late or miss my tee time. If I am really honest it will be that I will be called upon, or expected to play, at my old handicap of 2.

Before I went over to Honolulu I was very apprehensive and feared every time my credit card was used that it would bounce back at me. That fear was totally unfounded because there was lots of money in my account and I had a back up card on another account just in case.

Of course they didn't use credit cards in 1570 nor did they need any passwords - you were just who you were and a great deal would go on looks and clothes and of course confidence and demeanour.

In the later chapters you will read about my meeting the ghost of Neil Armstrong and going back in time with him to play golf. He wanted my help to do several things.

First to go and claim our prize for winning the competition in 1969 and that we did in spades thoroughly enjoying every moment.

He looked to me like a man of 35 in his prime and happy and confident and I am sure that I looked to him like a man of 27 just a few years younger that him also confident and in my prime. We were both wearing the clothes of 1969 with suntanned knees as an added bonus.

Those sceptics amongst you will say that it was all in my imagination and that is true but that may be the key to everything. Maybe everything is just part of our imagination and may need our imagination to act as medium or lubricator.

Why bother you may argue and I have several times thrown this book into the waste paper basket, which in my case of necessity is quite a large one. But then something stirs again like seeing Elon Musk on the Internet announcing his new Dragon 2 space capsule and I try again.

More and more of our daily lives in 2013 seem to be directed towards videos and games which are almost total fantasy - just as well because people seem to be being killed all the time in these games, and we would soon run out of people if it was real.

They have gone to a great deal of trouble making the fantasies as real as possible and in that they are brilliant. In fact if they weren't more brilliant than the rival game then they wouldn't sell any. All of them feed in to our imagination.

So maybe my imagination is better placed that I thought.
I find I can float out to anywhere I choose in the lovely gap between 7am, when the heating kicks in and wakes me up, and 7:40 am when the alarm goes off.

That is the best, and certainly the longest, 40 minutes in any day. It can go on for days while I am whisked away to the Panama Canal where I often meet Anna Botting, the lovely presenter of Sky News for lunch.

Chapter 9
Back To Hawaii

In late 2012 I began literally to dream more about the trip that I had in 1969 out to New Zealand and then Honolulu.

I started to dream about the golf I had played at the Navy Marine course in Honolulu with three strangers I met on the plane coming from Fiji to Honolulu.

We played together in a golf competition and won a prize which was to be flown over to the famous Mauna Kea Resort for a celebratory round.

I knew right at the start that one of the three was called Neil, but I can't remember anything about the others. I was living in Cape Town, South Africa, in 1969 and there was no television at all and we read little of international news in the papers.

I started to dream about one of the men I played golf with in 1969, and as each dream progressed I managed to put a little bit more of a picture together of this chap, Neil, who I had played with. That of course is the same name as my own and we joked about it if I remember right. Light hair and looked physically fit, as did his two colleagues.

I knew they were military people as every time I contacted the course where we played I was asked, "Are you military, because if you are not then you can't play, simple as that". I recall clearly that it was the Navy Marine course very close to Pearl Harbour that we played, and could almost walk from the airport.

As the days and months passed I began to think that it is was possible that the military man called Neil could be Neil Armstrong because at the time he was in training there in Hawaii, as is well documented. I mentioned this to my family, particularly my son, Andrew, who said that "You must go and retrace your steps and see if you can find for certain who the man was, and who the others were".

If it was Neil Armstrong that I had met in 1969 and the date was confirmed to be in July 1969 then that would prove that what everybody saw on television had to be pre-recorded and was therefore a hoax. But that was the only explanation.

After it was announced in August 2012 that Neil Armstrong had died, I started getting stronger messages drawing me there quite literally to play golf. I have been addicted to golf all my life and have had the pleasure of playing almost all over the world. A set of golf clubs is a passport and if you can swing the club reasonably well it is a pleasure.

There was also something else in that I had a whole raft of memories which have been suppressed just bursting to get out and it seemed to me that Neil was telling me that the embargo was now over and he could reveal all.

I wanted to get back to the days when I was off a handicap of 2, hitting the ball a mile and putting irons shots close to the pin, which I made look quite easy as they do on television.

I drew up an itinerary whose sole object was to get me safely and quickly to Honolulu and then rest up for a day or night, and then go to the Navy Marine Club to play again with the friends I had made in 1969. The more I planned it, the more excited I became.

I decided to stay at the Ohana Hotel, which is practically in Honolulu Airport and is within walking distance of the Navy Marine Course. Once I got there I was certain that Neil Armstrong would be there. "Why?" you ask. Simple. Because he was screaming that every morning in my ear.

I like aeroplanes and so I was looking forward to the trip. When you are settled in your seat and know that there is a nice meal to look forward to with some nice wine and of course a large Drambuie to finish - sleep is positively guaranteed. And that is what happened on the first leg out to Los Angeles. I was with British Airways, which helps, as they know how to look after you well.

No one can fail to be excited by the thought of Los Angeles with all its glitter and razzmatazz and I landed knowing that I had a boarding pass for the next hop to Honolulu and they simply don't take off if passenger Burns has not handed in his boarding pass and taken his seat.

I knew I had to clear customs and immigration in Los Angeles, my first port of call and I was feeling rather pleased with myself having obtained an ESTA pass, which everybody has to have to get into the States. I had been told about it by the Tranquillity Travel people in Bewdley who helped me put the

First serious itinerary for Hawaii

Day 1
Drive from Dormer to Premier Inn at Heathrow
Check Yeti in the long term car park   must be already booked and paid for
Dinner at Hotel   **early night Premier** 13 November Wednesday
Day 2
Up for breakfast early
Catch the shuttle to Terminal whatever   American Airlines Take off 940am
Check in by 740 am and go through security
Fly to Los Angeles 10 hours or so   **sleep on plane night of 14**
Day 3
Arrive at Los Angeles and go through transit (easier said than done)
Wait 2 hours
Take off for Honolulu 8 hours or so
Arrive at Honolulu   1915 local time   clear customs **gained 10 hours time**
Shuttle to Ohana Honolulu Airport hotel 15 minutes
Ask about 1969
dinner and **sleep Ohana   night of 14 november confirmed by Geoff**
Day 4
Up for breakfast
Go to Navy Marine Golf Course to play 9 holes in afternoon Ask about 1969
Back to hotel for **sleep Ohana   night of 15 November**
Day 5
Up breakfast
Take Hawaiian Airlines flight to Kona Int Airport
Hire car and drive down to Mauna Kea 25 miles
Check in to Mauna Kea Golf Hotel and book golf for next day
Explore in afternoon with your car possible ThisCave ThatCave
Dinner at Hotel   enjoy the luxury !! **Sleep Mauna Kea night of 16 November**
Day 6
Up for breakfast and get to first tee in good time
Play 9 holes at least   get lots of cards for boys back home
Lunch and sleep in hotel/car
Afternoon free for trip up to Observatory ThisCave ThatCave
Take car back to Kona airport
Fly Hawaiian airlines back Kona to Honolulu   HA307 leaves 8.05pm HA397 9.19pm
Back to stay at Ohana Hotel Honolulu **sleep Ohana night of 17 november**
Day 7
Up very early breakfast
Check in for return flight 515 it is so early takes 20 hours plus 10 gain back
Take off from Honolulu for Los Angeles 715 **then you lose ten hours back again**
sleep on plane 18 November
Day 8
Land Los Angeles
Clear customs
Take off for Heathrow   **sleep on plane 19 November**
Day 9
Land at Heathrow 12.00 local time clear customs
don't forget car land on 20 November

My boarding pass issued in my full passport name of Andrew Neil Burns

finishing touches to the itinerary.

I picked up my red suitcase and the wonderful golf clubs, which came as separate items, but they both arrived and I knew them both well.

"Did you pack these yourself?" I was asked. "Most certainly I did" and I was about to undo the rather splendid red ribbon I have round my case for identification purposes when the customs officer waived that aside. "What are these?" he asked, lifting up my half set of clubs, which is all I carry now on my 72 year old shoulders, but it is all I need and my skill and enthusiasm see me through.. "These are my wonderful golf clubs. I wouldn't travel without them," I told him.

I checked them in again and that was noted on my boarding pass and we were off. I made friends with some Scots people who reminded my that there was no food provided by the kind American Airlines people on internal flights, so I took with me some fruit juice and sandwiches, which were just enough to see me through.

The whole journey was going west into the sun and so we caught up with the clock arriving 10 hours earlier than our wristwatch so it was still light when we arrived in Honolulu. Also it was a pleasant surprise to find that there were no major immigration or customs control because this was just an internal flight within the USA.

So I waltzed through Customs to find the little shuttle bus with Ohana International Airport Hotel emblazoned on the side. "That will do me nicely," said I, as the chatty driver welcomed me to Hawaii. "Aloha" is the term for welcome and they make an art of welcoming you at every turn.

I had booked and paid for my hotel room already and so I checked in quickly and strode upstairs with a view to hitting the hay and catching up with the jet lag sleep required.

I was jolly hungry and noticed that breakfast was being served and I took advantage of this stroke of luck by tucking in. I could claim that this was all part of the planning process aided by the Tranquillity people, but suffice it to say, I had bacon and eggs and hash browns for the first time in a long time with lots of fruit juice - all natural juice - poured into my glass.

Off to my bedroom I went. I drew the door bang shut, checked the air conditioning was at 70, and off I went for a most welcome sleep.

I had a great bath when I got up. I got dressed into my golfing clothes, which I wear every week - long dark blue trousers and sufficient jerseys to keep me warm even when there is an early morning frost at Cleobury Mortimer.

I can discard them if the sun decides to come out as it very occasionally does. As we often have a little mud to contend with my shoes are often a little scruffy but serviceable nevertheless.

I am not sure how long I slept for but I had asked for a taxi to take me to the Navy Marine Club, which was my first port of call. I was expected by the Club professional David Chin.

I arranged with my taxi driver, who was originally from Vietnam, that he would take me first with great confidence to the course. We would later go to Waikiki Beach, which is the mandatory trip for all visitors to Honolulu. His eyes lit up because this would take us a while and run up a good tab on the taxi. We agreed a hundred dollars and we were both happy. I would see the famous surfing beaches where I understood their hero's statue could be seen.

I told him I was hoping to confirm that I had played golf at Navy Marine in 1969 and I was confident that I would be shown the visitors book where the three men must have signed me in as their guest.

Chapter 10
Welcome At The Navy Marine Golf Club

I walked round to the front of the club which I remembered well. As I did so I saw another golfer in his thirties walking towards me with a friendly welcoming gait . He was wearing the same outfit that I remember with the long shorts and matching socks that I recall from 40 years ago.

The hairs on the back of my neck started to rise as I realised that I was about to experience something extraordinary. Here was the man I wanted to meet and he was striding towards me apparently keen to make contact !!

He said, " How good to see you again!" as he strode to shake my hand. "I think we may have the chance to play again. I have spoken to David Chin. I see you are all kitted up ready to go".

And when I looked down at my own shorts they were the same as his - the very ones he had given to me on that first day.

I realised with some excitement that I was back in 1969 and just less than thirty years old. I strode with some confidence towards this other man who I could now observe in some detail. He was just turned thirty, smart casual with the look of a uniform to his dress and when I saw the others it seemed to be standard issue.

I was wearing the shorts I was so used to in South Africa with long socks and my knees were heavily tanned. I had been thrown back to my heyday in Cape Town and presumably if I was wearing the clothes my game would come up to match.

Now there was no doubt at all in my mind that this man had bumped me back to the time in 1969 when we had last played here. Happy memories. And I think he wanted to play again to relive those glory days. "Lets win again," he said, and I said, "I'll go for that". I realised that I was in my 1969 gear and so ready to play.

We carried on walking and I realised with some excitement that it was Mr Armstrong's ghost that was walking with me. We strode confidently round the corner. "Lets see if we can find Buzz because we need him on good form for his long irons. He's quite good at those" He asked the starter if the others

The author is photographed with David Chin, the Golf Club Professional at the Navy Marine Golf Club, in 2013.

were here and all he said was "Not yet, Sir, but we expect them soon."

In retrospect I think we were not likely to see them certainly as ghosts because they are still alive and as I keep telling myself I only see them afterwards as I was seeing this man beside me who must certainly be Neil Armstrong.

I carried on round a circle and I remember doing this very clearly as I took some photographs of those men already on the tee. I carried on round and when I got far enough to see my taxi again I looked down at my shoes and they were my regular twenty first century slip on black shoes - a little bit grubby I am rather ashamed to say. My taxi driver asked if I had been successful and I said "Most certainly, yes" because I had seen Neil Armstrong and been on the verge of seeing his two partners, but for two good reasons they not yet arrived and even if they had done so, I would not have been able to see them as ghosts. This firmed up everything and David Chin had recognised me and we had taken two photographs of our better sides!

The taxi driver set off to show me Waikiki Beach, which is one of the most

History at Navy Marine

famous surfing beaches in the world. Not that I planned to do any surfing myself!

My taxi man showed me the statue of the famous Hawaiian surfer who was the world champion. They had a statue way more than life size standing on the pavement near the beach. I was surprised and slightly embarrassed that I didn't recognise his name.

On reflection, the meeting with Neil Armstrong's ghost earlier was classic. I walked round a corner talking to him and then walking round further and noticing that he was thirty and was a similar age to me wearing clothes of that period. Then getting round the corner where he could see everyone in 1969 but I could only really see him and then coming round back in front of the clubhouse and it was all back to normal with my normal shoes and long trousers.

Let's think back to what he said because he was going to tell me something.

So after our sojourn into Waikiki I asked the taxi driver to go back and he pointed out to me "You are bound to be welcome because your name is in the visitors book!" So we went back (as I had nothing better to do) and this time as I walked round there was Mr Armstrong sitting outside having a drink with a satisfied smile on his face.

"I think we have done well enough to win," he cried, "thanks to all those chip shots you ran up close that must have saved us six shots or so".

I agreed, "Those are critical to a good score. But you chaps holed the putts of course," I joked, which was true of course and saved me the stress of holing small putts which you are very often given but you are not expected to miss.

"Come down and have a seat as the others are having a shower. I think we will have to make plans to go to Mauna Kea tomorrow. They will lay on a military plane for us I would imagine."

"Yes, I am looking forward to that," I said.

Just as he was getting ready to tell me more, he turned and I saw my taxi driver looking a little concerned round the corner. I got up said, "Excuse me" and went round to check he was OK. When I returned Mr Armstrong was gone and the steward told me that we had won and you had better be back here tomorrow sharp at 8:30am where you will be picked up.

I acknowledged what he said and went back to the taxi driver to take me back to the hotel. "Did you see the Visitors book?" he asked me and I had to say, "much better than that - I saw the man I played with and we won the competition again".

As I tried to gather myself I realised that I was already booked on the flight to Kona at 8.30 in the morning and prickles went up the back of my neck because I was flipping from 1969 to 2013 and back again with apparent ease. Maybe I will see them all on the plane tomorrow and I left it there.

The little shuttle bus took me in the morning to the terminal only half a mile as the crow flies and I already had my case and half set of clubs checked in and so I went to the exit gate waiting for the flight.

Chapter 11
Fly To Mauna Kea For The Prize

I could hardily catch my breath before we were on this little plane headed for Kona Airport. Forty minutes of pleasure away and on both sides of the little plane was the vista of beautiful scenery worthy of any Elvis Presley film.

Although it was a tiny plane, there was nevertheless an attentive airhostess who announced that we were about to land. We could see beside the tiny airport building a rather swish limousine sent by the hotel with the hotel name splashed across the sides which was almost keeping pace with us as we taxied up to the Airport building. Clearly we were expected and were going to get the right royal treatment.

The Mauna Kea hotel is one of the most expensive in that part of the world and that is why it was such a treat for us to go there as winners. Everything was laid on including having our clubs cleaned and our shoes polished and club cars all ready to go. The journey was all along Route 19, which is cut through the black lava fields formed by the lava cooling many centuries ago. The road took us 24 miles all the way from the airport to Mauna Kea Golf Hotel.

"Your car has been upgraded Mr Burns, apparently you need one to take four men and their golf clubs and we have just the job for you". And round the corner appeared a big Chevrolet Station wagon thing. Enormous is the only word I would have for it and it slid silently to a stop outside the Avis main desk. I was also rather pleased to see that it came equipped with a driver who took my clubs and added them to the others in the back. I noticed without saying anything that it was rather splendid set from Royal Cape with my membership badges and including the R&A badge in all its modest splendour.

I realised of course that this was a car sent by the hotel and we were being given the right royal treatment and Angus then reminded me it is quite easy to get to Mauna Kea, turn left go 700 metres toward to the highway, turn left again and go 24 miles and turn left again!

With that the driver piped up that he was aware of the route and could deal with it and I joked, "We have every confidence!"

We were surrounded by valets who were fighting to obtain the keys to drive it away and the tall elegant manageress of the club walked forward and said we already have a booking for you Mr Burns. "How did you know we were coming?" and I chuckled.

"That is called forward planning".

We drew up in their large turning circle outside reception. Porters and valets surrounded us. "Leave everything to them" said the hotel Manager, "and come and sign in". We all had to give our details as is normal in all hotels and we were each given a key with a very clear number on it and each set off for our rooms to change ready for our game. We all had a spectacular view from the balcony heading off for hundreds if not thousands of miles to the west possibly as far as China. We were four important individuals who were getting special treatment because we had won a golf competition and I don't think any of the staff knew anything about us other than our names. One of the valets came to fetch us to go to the first tee and it seemed he doubled up as the Starter. He was obviously under instructions to make our rounds as pleasurable as possible. The tee had been kept clear for the previous half hour and so we would not be held up by anyone and I presume the same would apply behind. That is so important in this day and age of slow golf, which everybody grumbles about but seems unable to do anything constructive about.

The dreaded 3rd across the bay at Mauna Kea.

The long beautiful beach at Mauna Kea Golf Hotel.

In the caddy carts we had an inexhaustible supply of brand new balls with the hotel motif and all we really had to do was play. As we enjoyed the Texas Scramble, we played again and some of the vistas on the course were spectacular and stunning.

After the game, we were invited to go and have a swim and a massage in the luxurious gym facilities, and I admit to a small snooze afterwards as I was massaged back into shape.

We then were asked whether we were going to dine in that evening and of course we were very keen to do so. Here are some menus and you will note that some of the dishes, particularly the best steaks, have to be ordered in advance. I asked: "Is that because they have to order the best steaks in Hawaii especially for us" and the Manager said that I had taken the words out of his mouth.

It seems the other three loved steak medium rare and I followed suit saying I will have another of those. The Manager said that would be a pleasure but I rather thought I heard him muttering they will have to go and kill another cow!

When eventually we ate later, the steaks were out of this world and tasted even better because we were not paying for them, it was part of our prize.

We had time in the late afternoon to go for a walk along the amazing beach, which seemed to go on forever and it was clearly a nice place for honeymoon couples with little nooks and crannies set off the beach for a little privacy.

The other three were keen to go in the water and practically dragged me in. It was so warm that we just dried out afterwards in the sun

They also had drinks trolleys taken along the path near the beach and we all had a beer from that, again knowing that it would be charged to our rooms. We were really having a splendid time, which of course was the whole object of the exercise.

I think it would have been a suitable venue for the team at John Menzies where we had a golf outing against the BBC, usually in St Tropez in France. Douglas Macdonald would have soon emptied the drinks trolleys and sent the boys back for refills!

We spotted one of the girls from the sauna department in a rather splendid bikini and that spurred my companions into some action and we all seemed to get separated. "See you for dinner!" I cried as I was dragged away by a tall girl in a red bikini. I couldn't possibly recall in this book what happened but

Ornate sculptured bunkers at Mauna Kea.

I think I remember that the bikini finished up in my suitcase as a souvenir. What happened in between I can only let you speculate.

After dinner we made sure we had early calls laid on and breakfast all together at the club where they do that sort of thing rather well.

When we got there the starter said that we have set the others to play with the Club Captain and the two Neils will be playing with our professional and his assistant and I realised that I was still in the aura of ghosts and of course I could see neither Michael nor Buzz because in 2013 they were still alive. Let's play Texas Scramble because that gives us the best chance and so we agreed to play for a pound, my Scottish pound, where of course we were favourites having two professionals in our team.

It was a real pleasure because there was no stress with the two pros hitting nice tee shots at the third over the water and so I had an almighty swing with my 5 wood and it sailed high and hard over the water to land past the pin and roll back only eighteen inches from the hole. I thought my partners would be pleased with me but like my brother they complained that I had left them a downhill putt! "Don't trouble me with that one please" said I and only relaxed when the Assistant Professional slammed it into the back of the hole. I swear it would have gone off the green onto the lava field below if it had not hit the back of the hole.

Sheer pleasure it was and even going into the bunkers was a pleasant experience because the sand was so fluffy and white that you could easily splash out close to the hole.

At the end of the match we thanked the pros for playing and collected our pounds from the others and then it unfortunately seemed to be time to go.

Chapter 12
Why Were You On A Commercial Airline?

I sat next to the other Neil, and took the opportunity of asking him, " Why ever were you on a commercial airplane? On that day in July 1969"

He replied, "We are surprised no one has asked us that before but I will tell you why and it is quite a long story in itself.

The original plan was to splash down in the South Pacific on the second day of our 8-day mission and then we would be taken by part of the team in the know to one of our ships into a medical isolation section where we would have every facility to keep us occupied for what was almost a week.

Well in those days it was an imperfect science and the person doing the calculations got it a bit wrong, and we overshot the point in the Pacific Ocean by some considerable way. We landed and no one was there to rescue us. We had done this many times on the simulator, so we were experts and we threw our training into full gear.

We knew how to open the outer door, but not before securing everything inside, so that if water got in we wouldn't sink. And because we had done it so many times under simulation, we were not fazed at all whereas we would have been panicking under other circumstances.

The craft was tiny as you know but it floated and we all got out of the craft onto the upper section and waited. What did the manual say? - "Wait to be rescued because we know exactly where you are".

But of course they didn't because we didn't know where we were and of course we had no way of communicating with anyone because theoretically we were on the Moon where we were far too far way to make any easy contact.

"When you panic you must panic slowly" was part of our training and we considered our options. We had no means of going anywhere because the craft had no outboard motor and so we just had to wait.

By extraordinary good fortune of course we had lots of provisions in the craft, like three days worth of rations and we tucked into a Moon breakfast with more than the usual relish. We all had wristwatches with us so we knew the tine but that was all of course there were no mobile phones then or computers so we were stuck.

We knew of course that if we were found by anyone then the whole game would be up and the Moon Hoax would become public, and we would be disgraced and we wanted to avoid that at all costs.

Well as luck would have it or, I suppose it was inevitable we were spotted by a fishing boat, which came along side. We were delighted that they neither spoke English (nor American) nor did they seem to recognise us at all. We had stowed away our spacesuits in the capsule, as it was of course quite warm.

It was just one man and his son and we thought they spoken in Fijian but we weren't certain. Thinking on the positive side we were saved and we must just ride our luck and so accepted their hand signals, which indicated they could give us a lift.

We had not the faintest idea where we were going and it might have been out of the frying pan into the fire. We headed off leaving the capsule sealed up but just floating and hoped that our boys had some way of tracking it down easily.

We then went back to the fisherman's island, which were part of the Fiji chain and were sheltered by this man, and slept under his roof for the night. They were all islanders speaking the same language, so we were safe for the meantime.

If this was Fiji then we were thousands of miles south of where we should be, but could still get back up to Honolulu where we were supposed to be collected, if only we could get to a bit of civilisation without alerting attention.

We started making some conversation with our rescuer and he seemed to be planning on selling us to the highest bidder who presumably would be on a bigger island, and we sort of went along with this.

After a good Fijian breakfast he took us on his boat and he knew exactly where to go - the big city and we realised that there was still a chance for us.

We had no money but we started bartering with our watches and by the time we saw a bigger island across the horizon we had already negotiated part of the way home.

Our new captain had a fresh spring in his step, and a nice watch on his wrist.

He took us straight to the beach close to the airport on Fiji where he landed us in exchange for my watch and a friendly handshake.

Our Captain knew some of the ground crew at the airport and obviously explained to them, that a wristwatch could be theirs, if they arranged things properly.

We still had two watches to go and when some of the natives there spoke English we negotiated flights to Honolulu using our two other watches. It seems some of them were crew, and we might pass as crew ourselves going back to Honolulu.

We were smuggled on to the plane having asked for it to be held up to get on and we just thought that it was possible we could make it back.

Well no one recognised us on the plane including yourself and although we were surprised and our egos rather deflated we realised if we just played the part of the crew returning then we could get into Honolulu.

We had no passports but the chap who got us the tickets also gave us crew passes so that we could both get on and off the plane without the usual checks. Remember then there was no need for security at all and you just had a paper ticket and boarding seat number.

We thought of course that anyone we saw would recognise us and blow our cover but as we chatted to you at the secret fruit juice department we realised that you didn't know who we were at all. The airhostess thought we were members of the crew getting a free ride home, and so we just held our breath.

When we arrived at Honolulu it was the twentieth and that was the day we were on television with the first giant step and of course everybody who had access to a television was watching. I had seen that scene so many times that we were fed up with it.

We decided that the safest place for us would be on the golf course where we often played and so we asked you to join us, and won the competition as a surprise bonus.

Of course by this time we had been onto our base and had clicked back into plan A and were taken by our team to the splashdown point with of course replacement spacesuits. We were ticked off unmercifully for losing the others but no one actually rocketed us for leaving the spacecraft capsule in the South Pacific Ocean.

When you started talking to people about publishing a book we decided we must get in touch with you and finish our game at Mauna Kea.

"That was quite a story wasn't it ", I said.

Chapter 13
Ellison Onizuka

Ellison Onizuka was the Hawaiian astronaut who made his first successful flight into space in 1985 on the Discovery shuttle completing 48 orbits of the earth. Tragically he was killed in the famous shuttle accident in 1986 when the Shuttle blew up, 73 seconds after take off.

There is a memorial or tribute to him at Kona near the Airport and after I had seen Elena at Splashers Grill. I had sufficient time to visit the memorial.

Whilst I was admiring the full description of his exploits, a young man walked up behind me and said "Ellison was a great man. What a pity he had to die in that way. I had to wait over 40 years for my release."

I realised this was the ghost of Neil Armstrong and it was perfectly possible for me to see him because I now realised that we had met here before of course in 1969.

This seemed to be the chance he had been waiting for to tell someone who would understand all his frustrations because he too had suffered terribly.

Neil Armstrong then poured out his woes in that he was embarrassed about taking accolades for being the first person on the Moon when he knew that he had never been there. "We were under military orders which we thought came straight from the President to play out the hoax. A small team from Hollywood came out to lot 151 in the Nevada desert to film them training. We spent hours doing all the landing and coming down the steps and making the footprint and raising the flag. The flag had to be held out stiff because there was no wind to do it. We jumped and hopped about on the dust to make it look as if it was very low gravity and when we asked why, the producers said that everything they did had to look realistic. They did the filming with lots of us and we thought that it would be for publicity films. We had to smooth back all the sand and dust after each shoot in case it had to be ready for the next day".

"These films were used of course as simulators and were excellent for training new astronauts to show how it should be done. Practically all our training was by way of simulations on the computer. We never thought for a moment that they would use the films and claim they were real".

As Neil was telling me all this, a man came up behind us just like another tourist or visitor to the Memorial and said "I agree with all this. I thought it was strange at the time that we had to film everything we did. We became quite used to it so it was second nature and if it didn't go exactly to plan we used to joke they will have to cut that."

I realised that this was Ellison as I recognised him from all the exhibits which surrounded us. Of course he was the same age as those photographs of him when he died and that too figured because I always see people at the age they were when they were at the place we met.

Ellison continued saying "I feel much the same as you, Neil, that I got all this adulation but all I did was get myself killed and that was no fun at all. Now of course I can tell you because you have an affinity with ghosts and I would like you to tell everyone what I am telling you."

"Have you not met Ellison before?", asked Neil, and I told him that I could only meet ghosts at the place where they were known to have been. That is why he can appear to us now because all three of us know that we have been here before.

"What should we do now?" I asked and he said "the answer is simple and you spotted it in your paper. We need to use springs, yes, springs, and set up a facility at Cape Canaveral or whatever with a huge array of resusable springs."

"Of course all springs are resusable but I am convinced that we can propel a small craft up to 5000 feet or so easily ready for Elon Musk's rockets to take over. Don't forget to ask Richard Branson for help because he has always been at the forefront of exciting adventures and invariably he has made great breakthroughs".

"Yes, I will do that" and that is the reason for publishing this book. "Why don't you also tell them about our other trips because I have given you the go ahead?"

Epilogue

On reading through the final draft for editing it strikes me that I have not brought my readers up to date with the developments from my previous two books.

In a Few Special Ghosts I Have Met there was a very strong connection to the Machin family of Droitwich. I visited the shop run by Machins at 69 High Street Droitwich where two chapters are set. By sheer chance, or some might say coincidence, I am going tomorrow to attend the Annual General Meeting of the company. I am company secretary and responsible for maintaining the Share Register and those of you who read my books would remember that we had a meeting at the Ripperage Inn where the latest Share Certificates issued were signed by Andrew Machin and David Harrison in 2001. We asked his two young sons to act and sign as witnesses and they should be at the meeting, 13 years older of course. Could we fleetingly go back to those years for some purpose?

In Haunted by Mary Queen of Scots I told the story of the wild gooseberry bush which I was asked to pick up at Wingfield Manor. I am glad to say it has now flourished and I have made a special place for it in the Mary Queen of Scots Garden where it has propagated profusely having plants now all over. For those of you who can't recall I was asked by Mary Queen of Scots to rescue this tiny plant which we have now established was 400 years old. It was all that remained of the plant which must have been sent down to Wingfield Manor where Mary was kept captive by the Earl of Shrewsbury on instructions from her Cousin Queen Elizabeth of England.

The leaves of this bush provided a relief for the pain of the arthritis in Mary's hands. She told me that she pushed the leaves under the fingers of her mittens and caused a welcome relief to the pain.

When I brought the plant back to a semblance of strength and some growth I took it with me to Buxton and much to the amusement of the hotel staff asked for permission to take it with me to the Mary Queen of Scots room where I was staying. I put it on the mantelpiece next door to her portrait and the hotel staff will confirm that we found a fresh growth of three inches of new light green shoots in the morning all towards their mistress.

Mary Queen of Scots Garden

Made entirely from plants and materials available in Tudor times
by Neil Burns

When I returned to Dormer I realised that I needed somewhere special to put the plant so that I could both observe and look after it. What better place than the Mary Queen of Scots Garden which I built in her honour at Dormer.

It is the exact same size as Marys Bower at Chatsworth where I sought planning permission to build it. I used only plants and materials which were available in Tudor times and constructed the garden using techniques used then. I obtained a modest number of Boxus plants and took cuttings from them to form the patterns and ornamental edging for the garden. Some thousands in all I would calculate.

Her earrings were made of Baggesens Gold and her eyes mainly heather from Scotland of course. Pools of water represent her hair. You can see from the aerial photograph that it was successful and is a proper tribute to her beauty. It can be seen on Google Earth and we open the Garden to the public possibly twice a year where my late wife Jennifer enjoyed acting as guide.

Another coincidence is that I am expecting today a delivery of 155 Nepeta plants, which are going to replace the Lavender in her headdress which have run their five-year course. By the time this book is published they should produce the wonderful blue cascade of colour for all to see.